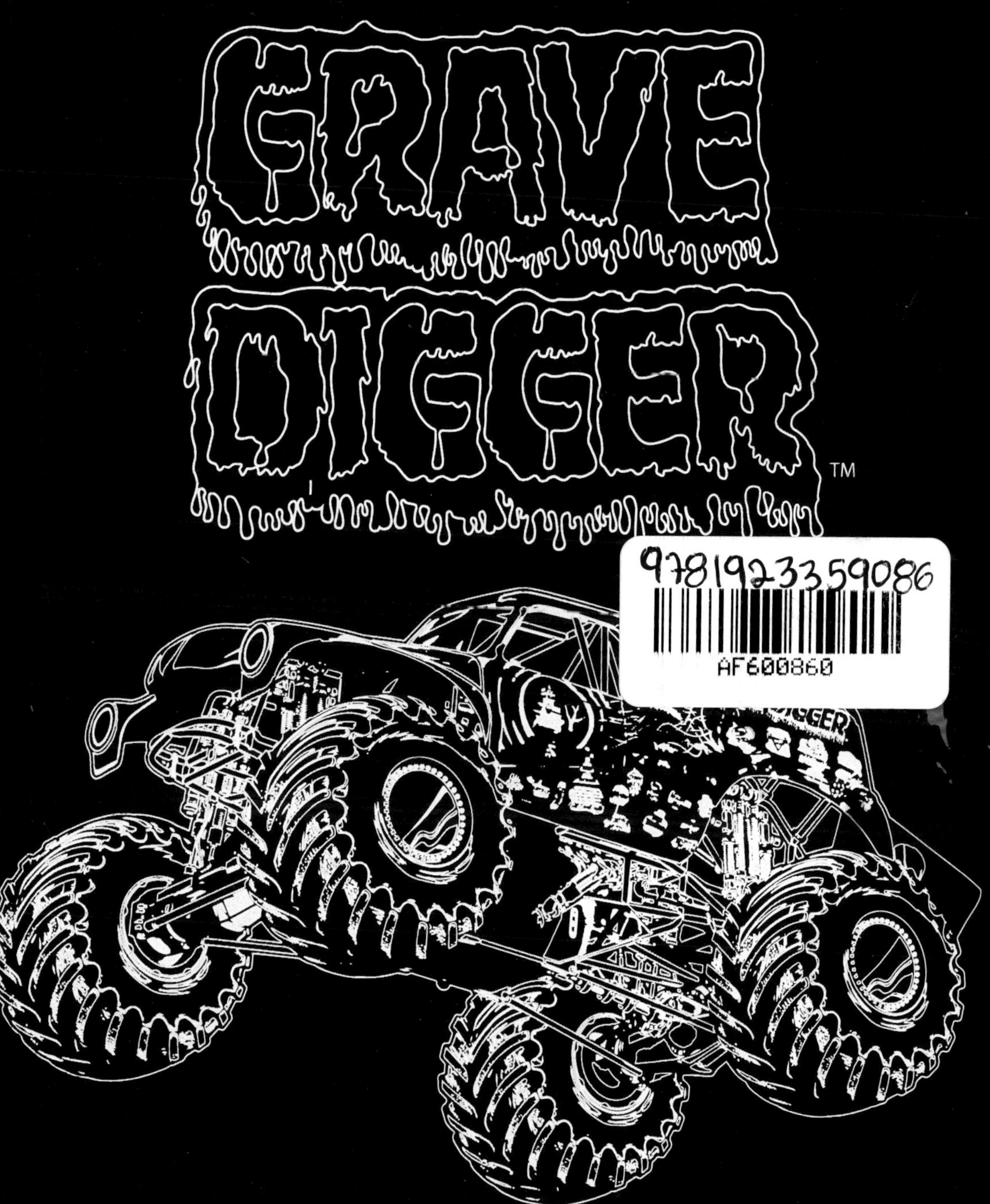

9781923359086
AF600860

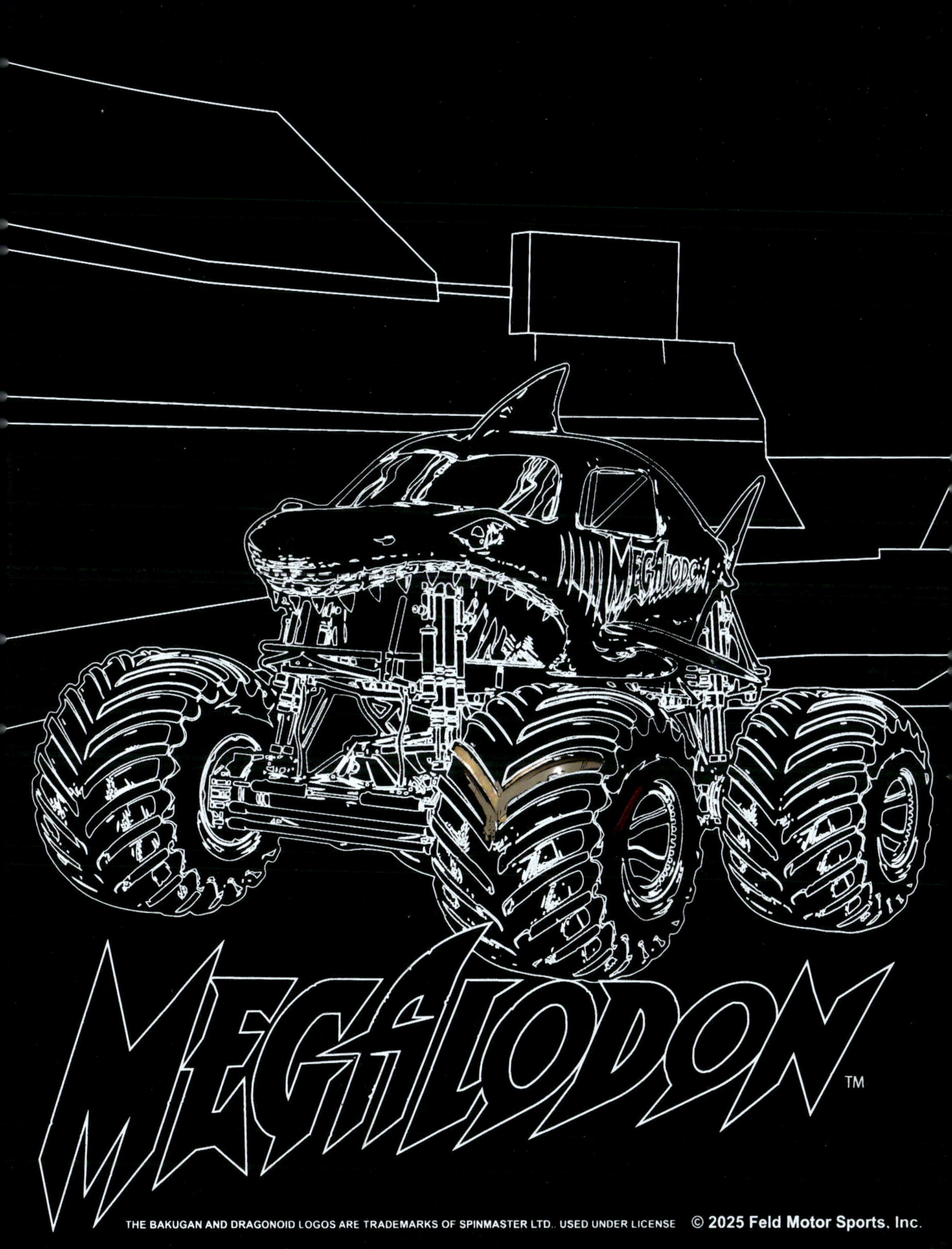
MEGALODON
MEGALODON™

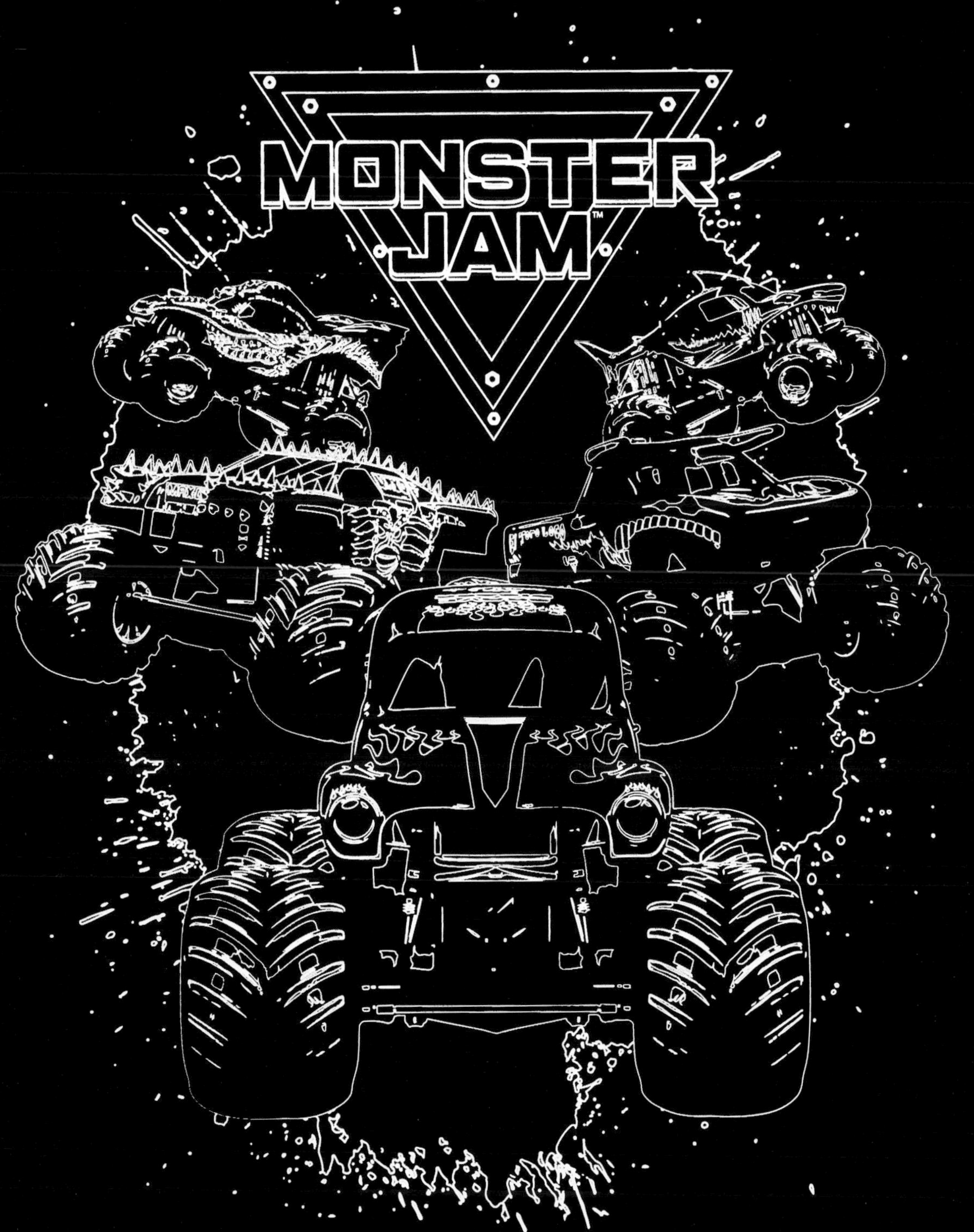
MONSTER
JAM™

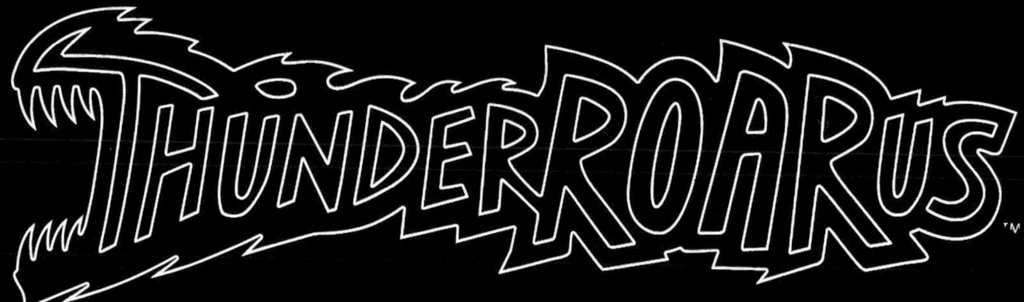
THUNDERROARUS™

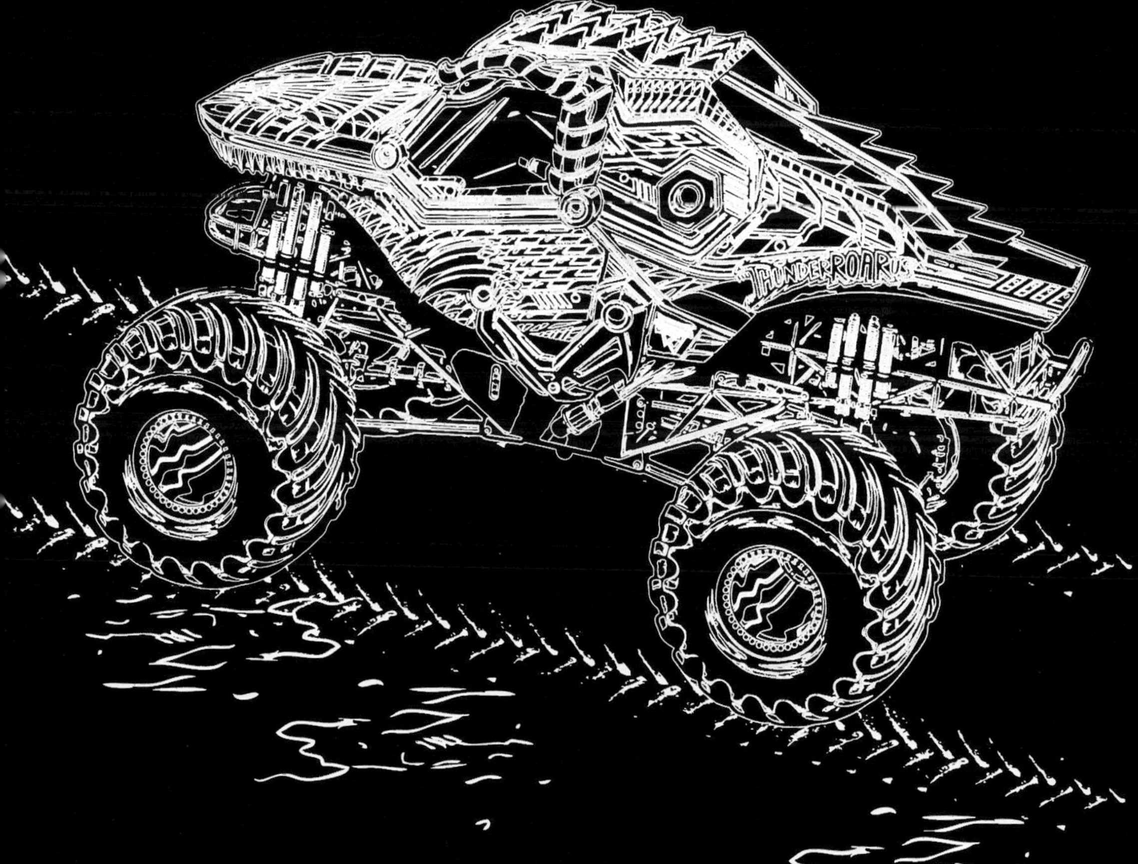

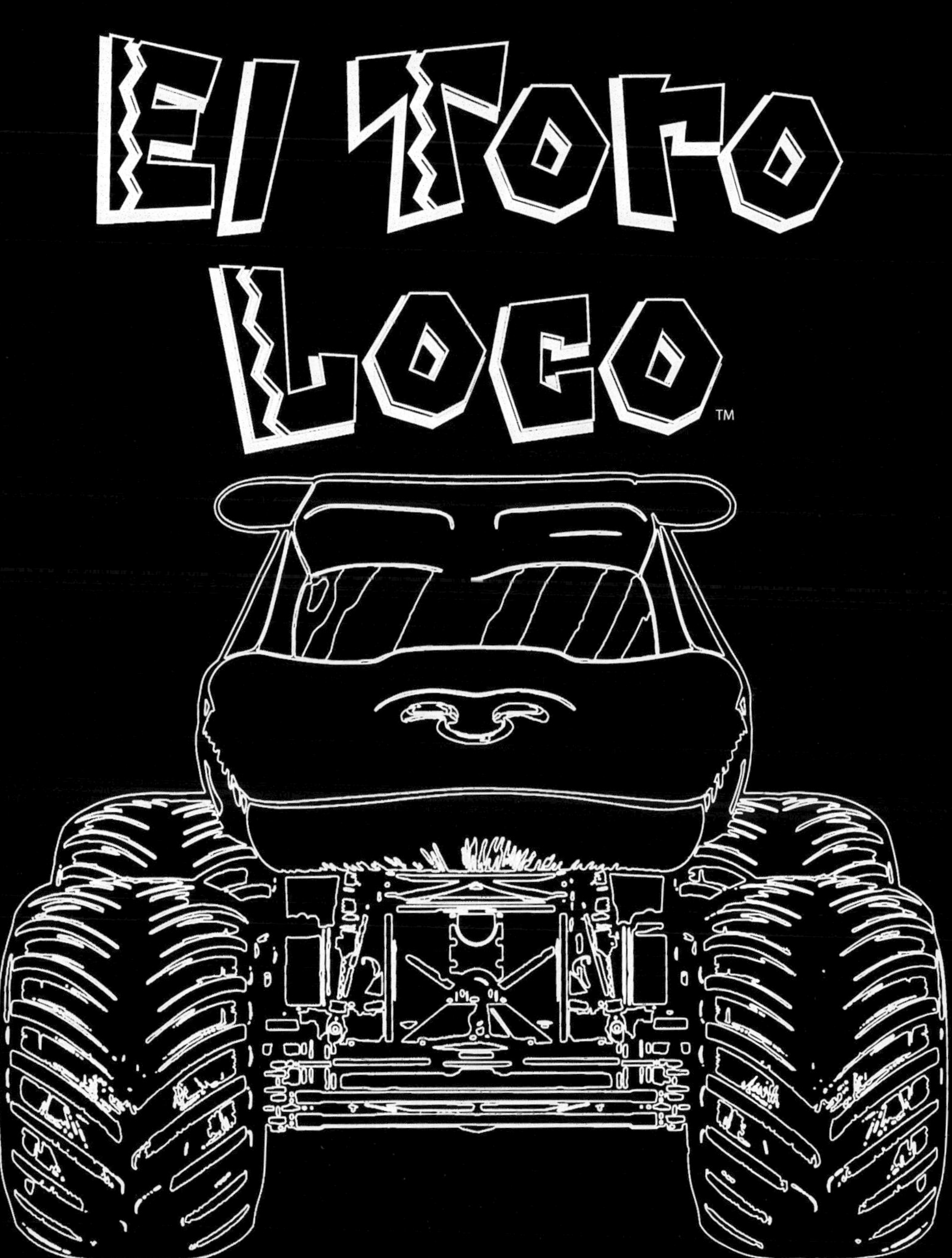
El Toro Loco™

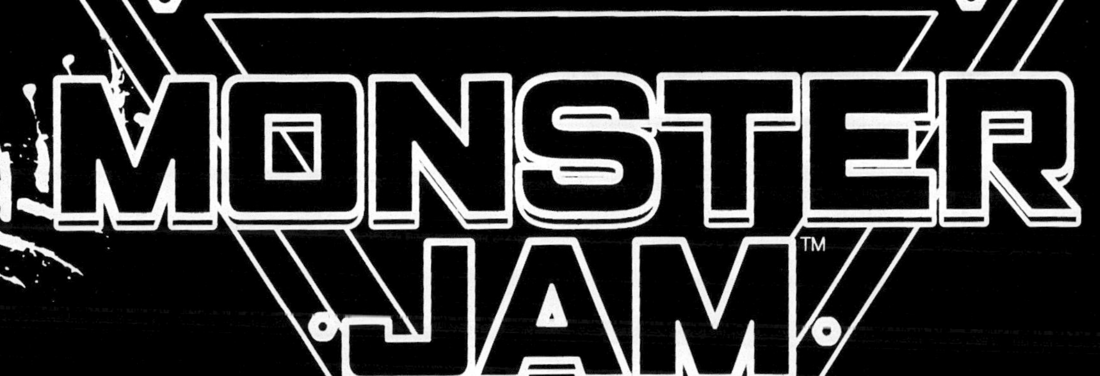
MONSTER
JAM™

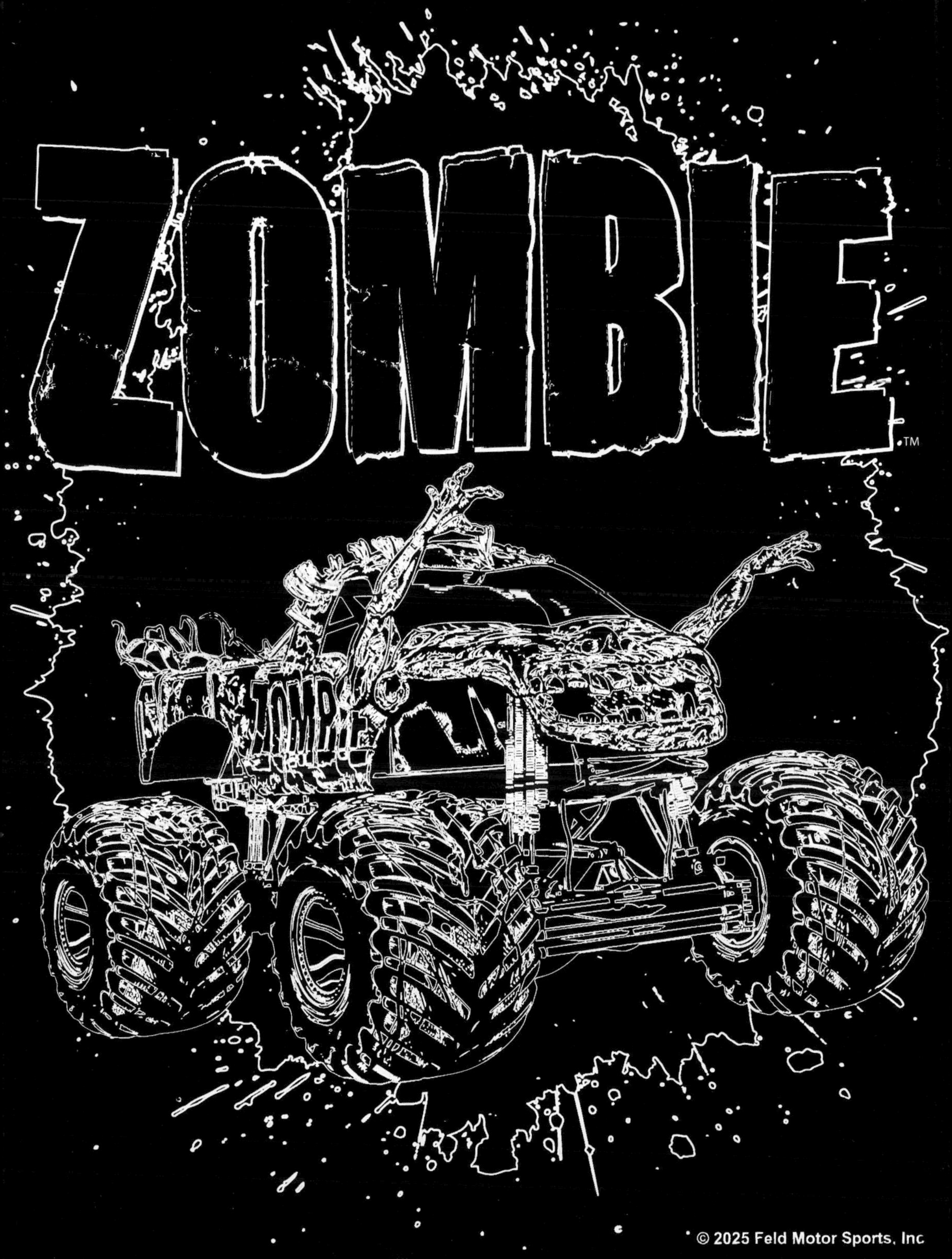
ZOMBIE™
ZOMBIE

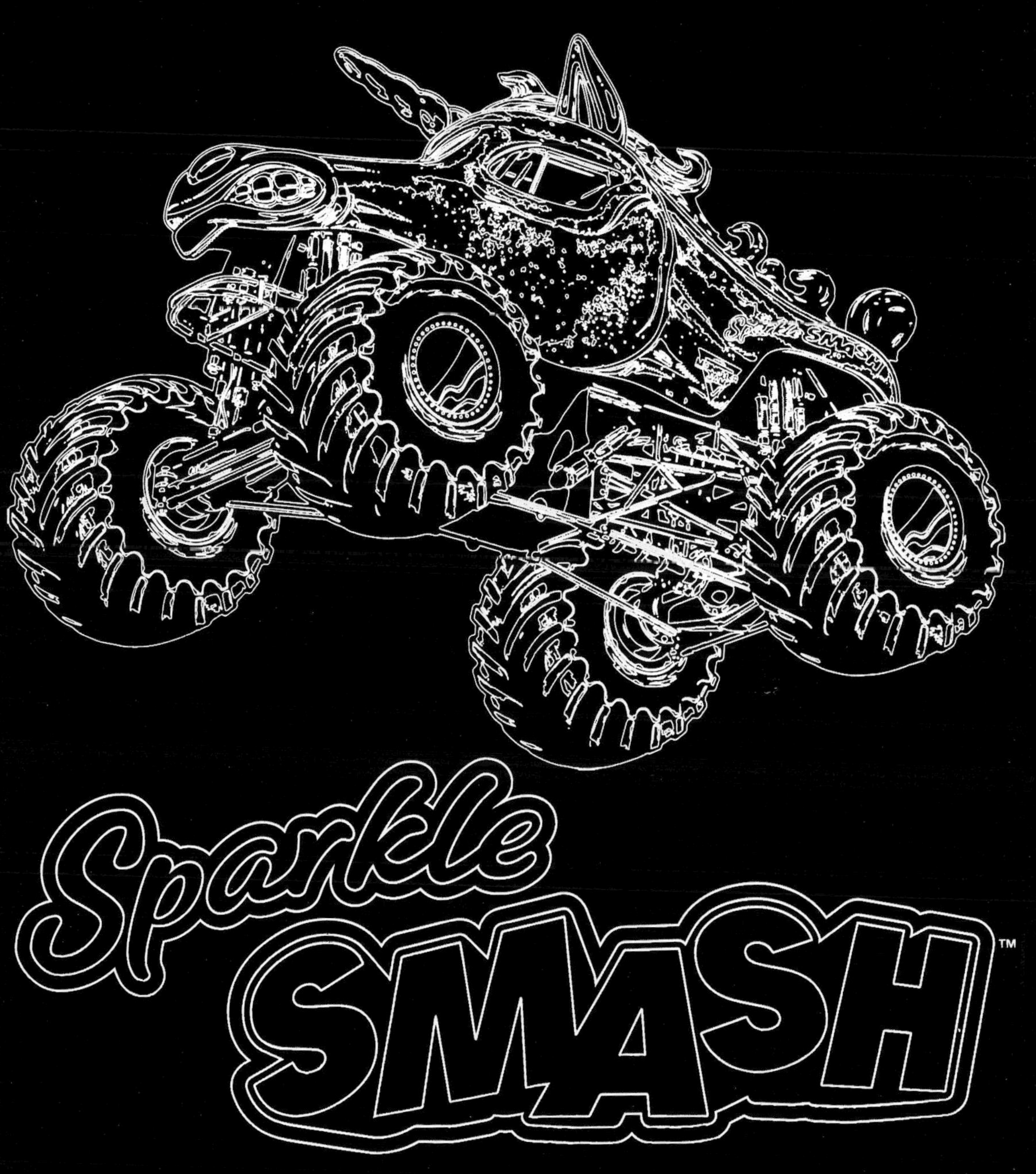
Sparkle SMASH
Sparkle SMASH™